I0814566

Rasmus Zepernick

Halloumi

Vegetarian Recipes Starring Your New Favorite Cheese

TOUCHWOOD

Contents

Preface

Recipes

The Favorites

Summer Salads

Comfort Foods

From My Family to Yours

Prefa

ce

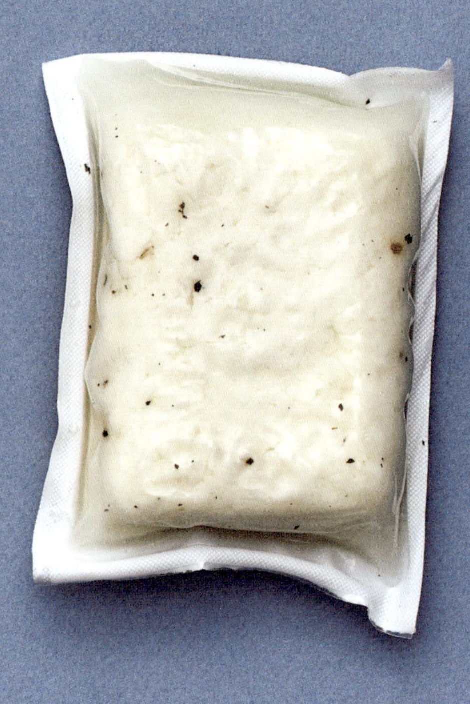

What is Halloumi?

Halloumi is to the Cypriots what feta is to the Greeks and brie to the French: a source of national pride.

This firm and savory cheese is a Cypriot delicacy, traditionally made by combining goat's and sheep's milk with mint—however, many manufacturers mix in cow's milk for practical reasons. Halloumi has a saltier flavor than other white cheeses you might be familiar with, as well as a slightly higher fat content. It's also rich in protein and calcium, both of which are essential elements of a healthy diet.

Halloumi has a high melting point of 275°F which makes it ideal for pan-frying or grilling, as it holds its shape even when subjected to very hot temperatures.

In recent years, its rise in popularity has made halloumi available in most supermarkets where you can find it next to other white cheeses such as feta and mozzarella. Halloumi-like products are also available in supermarkets, sometimes going by the generic name "grilled cheese" because authentic Cypriot halloumi can only come from Cyprus, just as authentic Greek feta can only come from Greece. I recommend buying real halloumi whenever possible, to ensure that you get the purest quality and best results with my recipes.

Introduction

The idea for this book came to me several years ago, when I stopped eating meat. I missed many of the recipes I used to make, and even though I no longer ate beef I still appreciated a good burger. At the same time, I found it difficult to adapt my eating habits to a vegetarian diet and didn't feel like changing them just because I no longer used that one ingredient. And so I began to think of ways to avoid giving up all the dishes I was so fond of. When my girlfriend introduced me to halloumi, it was as if all the pieces fell back into place: I could keep cooking the food I loved without meat. With this book, I hope to inspire more people to try halloumi, through a collection of recipes that range from well-known classics from the global kitchen, to family favorites and original creations from my own kitchen. Halloumi makes for a perfect meat substitute in my opinion, but it's also a wonderful addition to meat-based dishes. In fact, halloumi tastes great with almost anything and I would go so far as to say that many of the dishes I used to make have improved since I made the switch. That's why none of the recipes in this book include meat—even those that typically would—because I want to show how easy it is to use halloumi as an equally tasty substitute.

While most of the recipes in this book will likely look familiar to you, some might seem completely foreign. However, all of the recipes have one thing in common: They are designed to be simple and easy to make. There is nothing more frustrating than having to figure out a recipe that asks for ingredients you've never heard of, or requires you to stand in the kitchen for hours with a bunch of fancy kitchen appliances you might never use again. I wanted to show that almost any dish can be improved by adding halloumi, and that vegetarian cooking is so much more than bitter greens and salads—although I would be lying if I said I haven't included a few scrumptious salad recipes, with halloumi straight from the grill.

I have done my absolute best to ensure that each recipe uses as few ingredients as possible, because I often find impossibly long and complicated ingredient lists a pain to work with. That's why I've crafted each recipe to be simple and flavorful, so that anyone can experience the wonderful taste of halloumi. I hope you'll love it as much as I do. Enjoy!

Recip

es

The Favorites

Gorniksson's Bulgur Salad

Serves 2

The first time I tasted halloumi was through this dish. Without it, this book would've likely never come to be. The recipe originally comes from my wonderful mother-in-law, Ms. Gorniksson, and it remains one of my go-tos for an easy and delicious lunch or dinner at home.

1 cup dried bulgur
1 (540 mL / 19 oz) can chickpeas
½ cup sun-dried tomatoes (jarred)
½ bunch fresh parsley
1 (200 g / 7 oz) block halloumi
5 Tbsp oil from the sun-dried tomatoes
Salt and pepper

Begin by cooking the bulgur according to the instructions on the package, usually around 12–15 minutes.

While the bulgur is cooking, rinse the chickpeas and finely chop the sun-dried tomatoes and parsley—remember to rinse the parsley first.

Next, cut the halloumi into 8 equal-size pieces. Fry them in a pan until golden brown and crispy.

Once the bulgur has finished cooking, transfer it to a bowl along with chickpeas, sun-dried tomatoes, parsley, and the oil from the sun-dried tomatoes.

Mix it all into a salad. Finish by seasoning with salt and pepper to taste.

Serve the bulgur salad with crispy pieces of halloumi and enjoy!

Flatbread with Hummus, Avocado, and Pomegranate

Serves 2

The first time I tasted this halloumi classic was at a popular Lebanese restaurant in Copenhagen named Mahalle. This is the perfect starter dish for anyone who's looking for an easy introduction to cooking with halloumi. The degree of difficulty can be adjusted depending on whether you want to make the flatbread yourself or buy it ready-made. I usually buy ready-made ones, but if you're feeling adventurous I recommend finding a good recipe online and giving it a try. You can also use ready-made hummus, or follow my simple recipe below.

Hummus
1 (540 mL / 19 oz) can chickpeas
½ cup olive oil
1–2 cloves garlic
2 tsp lemon juice
Salt and pepper

Flatbread
1 (200 g / 7 oz) block halloumi
1 pomegranate
2 pitas or flatbreads
6 Tbsp hummus
1 avocado

Hummus
Drain the chickpeas and place them in a blender along with the olive oil, garlic, lemon juice, and a pinch of salt.

Blend until the desired consistency is reached.

Add more oil if necessary and season with salt and pepper to taste.

Flatbread
Cut your halloumi into 8 equal-sized pieces. Fry them in a pan until they turn golden brown and crispy.

Peel the pomegranate and pick out the seeds. Peel the avocado and cut it into equal-sized slices.

Once the halloumi is almost ready, heat the flatbreads in the oven.

Assemble your flatbreads by spreading hummus, sliced avocado, and freshly fried halloumi evenly across both. Finish by sprinkling with pomegranate seeds and serve while the halloumi is nice and hot. Enjoy!

The Saturday Sandwich

Serves 2

My girlfriend and I have started setting aside some extra time to cook whenever we're home during the weekends. On Saturdays we often make delicious sandwiches for lunch, and this one is my personal favorite.

1 bell pepper
2 slices good-quality bread
1 (200 g / 7 oz) block halloumi
2 eggs
¼ cup cream cheese
1 avocado
Pea shoots for garnish

Begin by rinsing the pepper and cutting it into large chunks. Place the chunks in a preheated oven with a drizzle of oil on top and roast them until soft and nicely charred.

Cut 2 slices of bread as thick or thin as you'd like. I prefer to use sourdough bread for this recipe, but feel free to use any other type of loaf.

In a heated pan, add butter or oil and toast the bread to your liking.

Cut the halloumi into 6 slices. Fry the slices in another pan until golden brown and crispy.

Once the bread has turned crispy, move it onto a plate and use the same pan to fry the 2 eggs.

Now it's time to assemble your sandwiches. Start by spreading a generous amount of cream cheese onto each piece of bread. Peel, cut, and mash the avocado and place it on top of the cheese, then add the fried peppers, halloumi, and finally the fried egg. Garnish with pea shoots and enjoy!

Halloumi Pita

Serves 2

Back when I used to live in central Copenhagen, I would often stop by a local shawarma place whenever I was coming home from work or a night out. I still think about their shawarmas more often than I care to admit, but I have managed to fill the void through developing this delicious pita recipe with halloumi.

Halloumi marinade

2 Tbsp olive oil
1 tsp paprika
1 tsp chili flakes
1 tsp cinnamon
1 tsp salt
1 (200 g / 7 oz) block halloumi

Raita

2 small tomatoes
½ cucumber
¾ cup Greek yogurt
1 clove garlic
Juice of ½ a lemon

Pita

¼ small red cabbage
½ red onion
2 pitas

Halloumi marinade
In a bowl, mix together all of the marinade ingredients and gently fold in the halloumi. Place the bowl in the fridge and let the marinade work its magic.

Raita
Rinse the tomatoes and cucumber, finely chop them, and transfer to a bowl. Add the yogurt, pressed garlic, and lemon juice. Mix well. Place the bowl in the fridge and mix once more just before serving.

Pita
Cut the marinated halloumi into thin slices and fry in a pan until golden brown and crispy. Finely chop the cabbage and red onion. Just before the halloumi is ready, heat the pita bread in the oven. Once ready, assemble your pita with the chopped fresh vegetables, raita, and halloumi. Enjoy!

Caesar Salad

Serves 2

Caesar salad is a true classic that's become a staple dish in both restaurants and home kitchens, including ours! It's a long-time personal favorite of mine, especially on those days when we need a quick and tasty dish for lunch or dinner.

Dressing

⅓ cup parmesan cheese
1 clove garlic
⅔ cup mayonnaise
2 Tbsp lemon juice
1 tsp Dijon mustard
1 tsp Worcestershire sauce
Salt and pepper

Salad

Bread croutons
1 (200 g / 7 oz) block halloumi
1 lb (500 g) romaine lettuce
¼ cup parmesan cheese

Dressing

Finely grate your parmesan and press the garlic. Place both in a bowl along with the other dressing ingredients.

Mix well. Place the dressing in the fridge until needed.

Salad

For the croutons you can use store-bought, or make your own in the oven with some leftover bread, olive oil and spices.

Cut the halloumi into chunks as big or small as you'd like. Fry them in a pan until golden brown and crispy.

Rinse the romaine lettuce, chop it into pieces and place it in a bowl.

Take out the dressing, add it to the bowl and toss it with the salad.

Arrange the salad on a plate and top with croutons and crispy halloumi.

If desired, grate some extra parmesan over your Caesar salad, serve and enjoy!

Halloumi Fries with Dip

Serves 2

I have yet to meet anyone who doesn't love a crispy French fry, and if you haven't tried halloumi fries yet you're in for a serious treat! These cheesy fries are some of the best I've ever tasted, and although I have stumbled upon them in the frozen aisle of some supermarkets the homemade version will always be superior—at least in my opinion.

Béarnaise dip

¾ cup mayonnaise
1 tsp mustard
1 Tbsp béarnaise essence (see recipe on page 87)
½ a bunch fresh tarragon
Juice of ½ a lemon
Salt and pepper

Fries

¾ cup flour
2 eggs
¾ cup panko breadcrumbs
2 (200 g / 7 oz each) blocks halloumi
4 cups neutral cooking oil
1 tsp salt

Béarnaise dip

In a bowl, mix the mayonnaise with the mustard, béarnaise essence, and chopped tarragon. Season with the lemon juice, salt, and pepper to taste. Place the bowl the fridge until serving time.

Fries

Place the flour, eggs, and breadcrumbs into separate bowls—one for each ingredient.

Cut the halloumi into long sticks about ¼ -inch thick. Bread them in the following order to ensure maximum crispiness: flour, egg, breadcrumbs, egg, breadcrumbs.

In a deep pot, heat the oil to approximately 350°F. Once the oil is ready, carefully add the halloumi fries and deep-fry them until golden brown and crispy. When they're ready, place them on a piece of paper towel to soak up excess oil.

Sprinkle the fries with salt and serve while hot with a side of dip. Enjoy!

Summer Salads

Watermelon and Mint Salad

Serves 2

The first time I had this delightful salad was at a café just off Bondi Beach in Sydney. It seemed so simple that I feared it only tasted as good as it did because I was traveling and soaking up the atmosphere. Fortunately, that wasn't the case, and this salad still tastes absolutely terrific, even on chilly days.

Mint dressing

¾ cup crème fraîche
1 clove garlic, pressed
1 bunch fresh mint, finely chopped
Salt and pepper

Salad

½ watermelon
1 cucumber
¼ cup cashews
1 (200 g / 7 oz) block halloumi

Mint dressing

Mix the crème fraîche with the garlic and mint (save some mint for the salad) and season with salt and pepper. Refrigerate until serving time.

Salad

Cut the watermelon into bite-sized pieces.

Use a potato peeler to peel the cucumber into thin ribbons.

Place the cashews in a pan and roast briefly.

Cut the halloumi into 8 slices. Fry them in a pan or throw them on the grill until golden brown and crispy.

Once your halloumi is ready, assemble the salad and serve with the fresh mint dressing. Enjoy!

Kale Salad with Orange Vinaigrette

Serves 2

Kale may not be the first thing that comes to mind when you think of summer salads, but the crispiness of the leaves combined with the freshness of blueberries and orange makes it a delicious treat to enjoy on a hot summer's day—or any day for that matter.

Orange vinaigrette
3 Tbsp orange juice
3 Tbsp olive oil
1 Tbsp honey
2 tsp Dijon mustard
Salt and pepper

Crispy kale
7 oz (200 g) kale leaves
3 Tbsp neutral cooking oil
Salt

Salad
10 oz (300 g) kale leaves
1 (200 g / 7 oz) block halloumi
½ red onion
⅓ cup blueberries

Orange vinaigrette

Mix all the vinaigrette ingredients in a bowl.

Crispy kale

Rinse the kale leaves, tear them into large pieces, and pat dry. Gently toss with oil and place them in an oven set to 250°F fan for about 15 minutes—check on them regularly to ensure they don't burn. Remove the leaves from the oil and sprinkle with salt.

Salad

Tear the kale leaves into medium-sized pieces and place them in a bowl.

Gently toss the kale with the orange vinaigrette.

Cut the halloumi into large chunks approximately 1 inch long/wide. Fry them in a pan until golden brown and crispy.

While the halloumi is cooking, slice the red onion into rings. Rinse your blueberries and cut them in half.

Once the halloumi is ready, it's time to assemble your salad. Start with fresh kale at the bottom, then add crispy kale, halloumi, and red onion. Sprinkle blueberries on top, serve, and enjoy!

Grilled Asparagus and Strawberry Salad

Serves 2

I can hardly imagine a summer in Denmark without strawberries, so I knew I had to include this salad. The combination of grilled asparagus, halloumi, and strawberries topped with balsamic glaze is nothing short of magical.

Balsamic glaze

¾ cup balsamic vinegar

Salad

⅛ cup pine nuts

10 oz (300 g) lamb's lettuce (corn salad)

1 bunch asparagus

1 pint (350 g) strawberries

1 (200 g / 7 oz) block halloumi

Balsamic glaze

To make the glaze, simply pour the balsamic vinegar into a pot and let it boil until it thickens and the liquid is reduced to about half. Put it in a bowl and refrigerate until serving time.

Salad

Toast your pine nuts in a pan until they turn golden.

Rinse the lettuce, asparagus, and strawberries and pat dry.

Cut the strawberries in half and place in a bowl along with the lamb's lettuce.

Cut the halloumi into 6 equal-size slices.

Turn on your grill and add asparagus and halloumi slices. Cook the asparagus until tender and the halloumi until it turns golden brown and crispy.

Serve the grilled asparagus and halloumi tossed salad, pine nuts, and balsamic glaze. Enjoy!

Fresh Peach Salad

Serves 2

This is another must-try summer salad with tasty grilled peaches and halloumi.

Normally I would use fresh peas for this salad, but the picture for the dish was taken during wintertime when fresh peas were impossible to come by, so I served it with cucumber ribbons instead—you can use either depending on your preference.

Dressing

3 Tbsp olive oil
2 Tbsp lemon juice
1 tsp honey

Salad

½ cup dried bulgur
3–4 peaches
1 bunch fresh parsley
3 oz (100 g) fresh peas (in shells)
1 (200 g / 7 oz) block halloumi
Salt and pepper

Dressing

To make your dressing, simply mix all three ingredients together in a bowl.

Salad

Cook the bulgur according to the instructions on the package, usually for 12–15 minutes.

Meanwhile, cut your peaches into bite-sized pieces so they're ready to go on the grill along with your halloumi.

Rinse and finely chop the parsley. Shell your peas (or peel your cucumber into thin ribbons).

Cut the halloumi into slices and cook them on the grill along with the peaches. Cook until the cheese has turned golden brown and crispy and the peaches are lightly charred and tender.

Toss the grilled peaches and halloumi with the bulgur, peas or cucumber, and dressing. Season with salt and pepper. Serve and enjoy!

3 Summer Skewers

Serves 2

Grilled skewers have been a summer staple as far back as I can remember, and for good reason: they're easy to make and the possible combinations are endless. I've included three of our favorites below.

Red pepper sauce
4 red peppers
2 cloves garlic, peeled
½ cup pine nuts
4 Tbsp olive oil

BBQ marinade
1–2 cloves garlic
½ cup ketchup
1 Tbsp balsamic vinegar
2 Tbsp brown sugar
1 tsp paprika
1 tsp salt

Garlic oil
4 cloves garlic
⅓ cup neutral cooking oil

Red pepper sauce

Cut the peppers into large chunks and place them skin-side up on a baking tray along with the cloves of garlic.

Brush the peppers and garlic with oil.

Heat your oven to 500°F and use the broil function to cook the peppers and garlic until the skin is nicely charred.

Once cooked, place them in a bowl with a lid on. Allow them to cool before peeling off the skin.

Mix peppers and garlic with pine nuts and olive oil, adjusting the consistency with oil along the way.

Season with salt and pepper to taste.

BBQ marinade

Peel and press the garlic and mix it in a bowl along with the other marinade ingredients.

Garlic oil

Crush the garlic cloves and mix with the neutral cooking oil of your choice.

Continued...

…continued

Squash skewers
1 squash
1 red bell pepper

Tomato skewers
12 oz (350 g) cherry tomatoes

Carrot skewers
2 carrots
1 red onion

2 (200 g / 7 oz each) blocks halloumi, cut into square chunks

Squash skewers

Using a peeler, peel the squash into long strips. Cut the bell pepper into 1-inch square pieces.

Assemble the skewers by alternately threading squash, peppers, and halloumi on skewers. Finish by marinating them in the garlic oil.

Tomato skewers

Rinse the cherry tomatoes and assemble the skewers by alternately threading tomatoes and halloumi chunks.

Carrot skewers

Cut or peel the carrots into very thin slices.

Cut the red onion into thin squares about the same size as the carrots.

Assemble the skewers by alternately threading carrots, onion, and halloumi. Finish by marinating the skewers in the BBQ marinade.

Once all skewers have been assembled and marinated, it's time to turn on the grill.

Grill the skewers until the vegetables have softened and charred and the halloumi has turned golden brown and crispy.

Serve with the red pepper sauce and enjoy!

Potato Salad with a Modern Twist

Serves 2

Potato salad is often associated with heaps of heavy sour cream and mayonnaise, but this version contains a few more greens and a lighter dressing that brings out all the different flavors. If you want to include crème fraîche, feel free to add some to the delicious summer dressing.

Herbal oil
Handful of thyme
Handful of basil
Handful of parsley
2¼ cups neutral oil

Summer dressing
½ cucumber
10 mint leaves
½ cup yogurt
Salt

Salad
1 lb (500 g) small potatoes
3½ oz (100 g) arugula
3½ oz (100 g) fresh peas
1 (200 g / 7 oz) block halloumi
2 Tbsp parmesan

Herbal oil

Make the herbal oil by blending the thyme, basil, and parsley with the oil.

Summer dressing

Grate the cucumber and use a clean kitchen towel to wring out excess liquid. Chop the mint leaves and mix with the shredded cucumber and the yogurt. Finish the dressing by seasoning with a little salt.

Salad

Boil the potatoes until tender and leave to cool.

Rinse the arugula and shell the fresh peas.

Cut the halloumi into 1-inch squares and fry them in a pan until golden brown and crispy.

Once the potatoes have cooled, cut them into bite-sized pieces and toss in the herbal oil along with the arugula and peas.

Plate the salad with crispy halloumi and summer dressing. Grate a few large pieces of parmesan on top and enjoy!

Bean Salad with Pesto

Serves 4

It may seem very simple, but the combination of beans with piquant pesto is nothing short of magical, and the halloumi serves as a savory cherry on top.

Pesto

1½ Tbsp pine nuts
1 bunch fresh basil
2 cloves garlic
¼ cup grated parmesan
3½ Tbsp olive oil
Salt and pepper

Salad

½ lb (250 g) cooked chickpeas
5 oz (150 g) spinach leaves
½ lb (250 g) cooked white beans
1 lb (500 g) green beans
1 (200 g / 7 oz) block halloumi

Pesto

Mix all the pesto ingredients together using a blender. Season with oil, salt, and pepper to taste.

Salad

First, roast your chickpeas in the oven. Turn the oven to 400°F fan, toss the chickpeas in a bit of olive oil, and place them in the oven for about 25 minutes. If you want to add more flavor, sprinkle some paprika on top before roasting.

Rinse the spinach leaves and white beans and place both in a bowl.

In a pot, boil your green beans in lightly salted water for around 3 minutes.

Cut the halloumi into chunks as big or small as you'd like. Fry them in a pan until golden brown and crispy.

Meanwhile, mix the other ingredients (except for the chickpeas) in with the pesto.

Once the halloumi is ready, serve it on top of the salad along with the crispy chickpeas and enjoy!

“Greek” Salad

Serves 2

I was tempted to call this a Cypriot salad rather than Greek. However, in many ways this dish is identical to the classic Greek salad we all know and love, the only major difference being that the traditional feta cheese has been replaced with halloumi.

1 (200 g / 7 oz) block halloumi
½ red onion
¼ lb (250 g) tomatoes
1 green pepper
½ cucumber (optional)
½ cup black olives
Olive oil
Salt and pepper
Dried oregano

Begin by cutting your halloumi into 1-inch chunks. Fry them in a pan until golden brown and crispy.

Meanwhile, peel and chop the red onion into small pieces. Rinse your other vegetables and chop them into large bite-sized pieces.

Cut the olives in half and mix them with the vegetables.

Toss everything with olive oil and finish by adding the salt, pepper, and dried oregano to taste.

Serve with crispy halloumi on top and enjoy!

Grilled Cabbage and Carrots

Serves 2

Nothing beats a salad with freshly grilled vegetables, and most of the ingredients in this recipe are prepared by simply throwing them on the grill. It just doesn't get much better—or easier—than that.

Hummus

1 (540 mL / 19 oz) can chickpeas
½ cup olive oil
1–2 cloves garlic
2 tsp lemon juice
Salt and pepper

Garlic oil

5 cloves garlic
¼ cup neutral cooking oil

Grilled cabbage and carrots

10 carrots
½ medium green cabbage
1 (200 g / 7 oz) block halloumi
½ cup parmesan cheese, grated
¼ cup walnuts
½ lemon
Salt and pepper

Hummus

Begin by draining the canned chickpeas. Place them in a blender along with olive oil, garlic, lemon juice, and a bit of salt.

Blend until the hummus has reached the desired consistency, adding more olive oil as needed. Finish by seasoning with salt and pepper to taste.

Garlic oil

Crush the garlic and mix with the neutral cooking oil.

Grilled cabbage and carrots

Slice your carrots in half lengthwise. Cut the cabbage into 4 equal-size pieces.

Coat carrots in the garlic oil and cut the halloumi into large triangles.

Next, place the cabbage and carrots on the grill—check on them regularly to ensure they don't burn before they're cooked through. Add the halloumi to the grill shortly after.

Once the vegetables are tender and the halloumi has turned golden brown and crispy, remove from the grill.

Now it's time to plate your salad. Shred some parmesan cheese and sprinkle it on top of the dish, along with walnuts and a drizzle of lemon juice. Place a dollop of hummus on the side, serve and enjoy!

Comfort Foods

Burgers

Serves 2

In recent years, burger restaurants of all kinds have started popping up on street corners in Denmark, each one better than the last. When I make my own burgers at home, I tend to be heavily inspired by my favorite local restaurants, and so far no other place does it for me like the Gasoline Grill in central Copenhagen. This recipe includes a dressing inspired by their delicious burger sauce.

Dressing (Gasoline sauce)
4 Tbsp mayonnaise
½ Tbsp ketchup
1 tsp Worcestershire sauce
2 Tbsp finely chopped pickled cucumbers
1 tsp paprika
Pepper

Burger
1 (200 g / 7 oz) block halloumi
½ head iceberg lettuce
½ red onion
1 large tomato
10 slices pickled cucumber
2 brioche buns

Dressing

Make the dressing by mixing all the ingredients in a bowl. Place it in the fridge until serving time.

Burger

Cut the halloumi in half so that you get 2 equal-size "steaks." Fry them in a pan until golden brown and crispy.

Rinse the iceberg lettuce and cut the red onion into rings.

Cut the tomato and pickled cucumbers into thin slices.

Heat the burger buns in the oven or in a pan.

Now it's time to assemble your burgers. Begin by spreading some of the dressing onto the bottom half of the buns. Next add the lettuce, crispy halloumi, more dressing, tomatoes, pickled cucumbers, and red onions before finishing with the top half of the bun. Serve and enjoy!

Pizza Quattro Formaggi

Serves 2

Pizza is my ultimate comfort food, and I am not ashamed to say that I've tried nearly every pizza out there—from fully loaded Meat Lover's to the world's best Margherita. When I have to make pizza at home, I almost always go for Quattro Formaggi. Some might be upset by the fact that I have left out Gorgonzola from this recipe, but that's just a personal preference of mine. If you love Gorgonzola, feel free to replace one of the other cheeses with it.

2 portions pizza dough
1 can pizza sauce (I use the brand Mutti)
1 (200 g / 7 oz) block halloumi
½ cup parmesan
2 cups grated North Sea cheese or Gouda
1½ cups fresh mozzarella
12 fresh basil leaves

Tip: If you want fresh pizza dough without having to make it yourself, many pizzerias offer their dough for sale.

Begin by preparing your pizza dough, whether homemade or bought, by rolling it out as flat and round as possible.

Spread an even layer of pizza sauce on top and place the dough in the oven for 7 minutes at 400°F.

Meanwhile, grate the halloumi, parmesan, and North Sea or Gouda cheese and cut the mozzarella into small chunks.

Remove the baked pizza dough from the oven and turn the temperature up to 450°F.

Spread each of the cheeses evenly onto the pizzas and place them in the oven once more.

Bake until the edges of the crust have turned crispy and the cheese has melted, around 15 minutes. I prefer a very crispy crust, but you might prefer to bake it for a shorter amount of time.

Finish by sprinkling the pizzas with the fresh basil leaves.

Serve and enjoy!

Quesadillas

Serves 2

For years, my experience with Mexican cuisine was pretty much limited to nachos, but that changed on a fateful night when one of my friends invited me over for quesadillas and made me realize just how amazing Mexican cuisine is.

Harissa (chili paste)
2 fresh chili peppers
2 bell peppers
2 Tbsp olive oil
1 tsp paprika
2 Tbsp tomato purée
1 tsp cumin
4 cloves garlic
Salt

Guacamole
1 tomato
2 avocados
2 Tbsp crème fraîche
1–2 cloves garlic, pressed
Juice of ½ lemon
Salt and pepper

Quesadillas
1 (200 g / 7 oz) block halloumi
1 small red onion
8 small tortillas

Harissa

Cut the chili and bell peppers in half. Place them on a baking sheet skin-side up and drizzle with olive oil.

Heat the oven to 500°F on the broiler setting and bake until the peppers are slightly blackened on top.

Place the peppers in a bowl with a lid on. Leave them to cool slightly before peeling off the skin.

Mix in with the other harissa ingredients and season with salt and pepper to taste.

Guacamole

Finely chop the tomato. Peel and mash your avocados and mix both with sour cream and garlic in a bowl.

Season to taste with the lemon juice, salt, pepper, and possibly one more clove of garlic. Refrigerate.

Quesadillas

Thinly slice the halloumi or grate it on a cheese grater and cut the red onion into thin rings.

Spread harissa, onion rings, and halloumi onto 4 tortillas and place another tortilla on top of each.

Heat a pan, add oil, and fry the quesadillas one at a time. Place a smaller pot lid on top of the quesadillas to keep them lying flat. They should be fried on both sides until they have turned crispy and the cheese has melted.

Once they're ready, simply serve and enjoy!

Risotto

Serves 2

Lately, my girlfriend and I have made risotto whenever we want to treat ourselves, because it doesn't take long to make and you can easily swap out many of the ingredients to suit your tastes. We often end up making this version because I'm crazy about halloumi, and my girlfriend is equally crazy about mushrooms.

½ lb (250 g) chanterelle mushrooms
2 shallots
1 clove garlic, pressed
1⅔ cups risotto rice
¾ cup white wine
4 cups vegetable broth
1 (200 g / 7 oz) block halloumi
¾ cup grated parmesan
2 Tbsp butter
Salt and pepper

Begin by cleaning your chanterelle mushrooms and cutting them into large chunks. Fry the mushrooms in a pan with butter and set aside.

Finely chop the shallots and sauté them in a pot or large skillet along with some oil and the pressed garlic. Add the rice and sauté for a few more minutes.

Next, add the white wine and heat it until it evaporates.

Once the wine has evaporated, slowly add the broth.

Cook the rice in the broth for 15–20 minutes or until broth is absorbed and the rice is tender.

Meanwhile, cut the halloumi into small pieces and fry them in another pan until golden brown and crispy.

As soon as the rice has finished cooking, add the parmesan, butter, most of the fried mushrooms, and halloumi to the pot.

Mix together, season with salt and pepper to taste, and serve immediately.

Garnish with the remaining mushrooms and enjoy!

Ravioli with Sweet Potato

Serves 2

If this is your first time making your own ravioli, don't fret if they don't turn out exactly as you would expect. It has taken me several tries to get them right and I still find myself struggling with them from time to time—but I promise, it's worth it.

Dough

2 cups durum flour
3 eggs

Filling

2 sweet potatoes
1 (200 g / 7 oz) block halloumi
1 clove garlic
½ cup mascarpone cream
¼ cup shredded parmesan cheese
1 egg yolk
Salt and pepper

Butter sauce

1 shallot
½ cup butter
8 sage leaves

Dough

Start by preparing the ravioli dough ahead of time. It needs to sit in the fridge for at least 20 minutes, but I suggest making it a day in advance.

Place durum flour on a clean work surface. Form a hole in the middle of the flour and crack the eggs into it. Mix the flour and eggs and knead until you have a smooth dough. Wrap up the dough and place it in the fridge until it needs to be rolled out.

Filling

Peel the sweet potatoes and boil them in a pot of lightly salted water until tender.

Cut the halloumi into very small chunks. Fry them in a pan until golden brown and crispy.

Let the cooked sweet potatoes cool in the pot. Press the garlic clove and add it to the pot along with the rest of the ingredients. Mash it all together and finish by seasoning with salt and pepper to taste.

Continued…

...continued

Now it's time to put together the ravioli. Remove the dough from the fridge and roll it out as thinly as possible. Divide it into 2 equal-size sheets.

Add your filling to one of the sheets by placing it in small mounds. The amount depends on how many ravioli you'd like to make.

Next, place the other sheet on top and cut out the ravioli using a cutter or a small glass. Remove them quickly once cut to keep them from sticking to the work surface.

Bring a saucepan of salted water to a boil.

Butter sauce

Prepare the butter sauce before you begin cooking the ravioli.

Finely chop the shallot. Heat a large skillet or pot, add butter and the shallot, and sauté. Add the sage leaves and continue to sauté until the butter has melted.

Finally, add your ravioli to the pot of boiling water and cook for 3 minutes.

Serve the cooked ravioli immediately along with the butter sauce and enjoy!

Lasagna

Serves 4

I don't know what I love most about lasagna—the fact that it tastes amazing no matter what you put in there or that there are always leftovers. My lasagna consumption peaked back when I was studying, and I always made a huge batch that lasted me several days. This recipe is only meant to cover one meal, but I guarantee it will make you come back for more!

Tomato sauce

1 onion
2 cloves garlic
2 Tbsp tomato purée
2 Tbsp chopped thyme
2 (540 mL / 19 oz) cans chopped tomatoes
1⅔ cups vegetable broth
1 squash

Béchamel (white) sauce

2 Tbsp butter
4 Tbsp wheat flour
2 cups milk
Nutmeg, grated
Salt and pepper

Lasagna

2 (200 g / 7 oz each) blocks halloumi
1 pack fresh lasagna sheets
¾ cup grated mozzarella cheese
Salt and pepper

Tomato sauce

Begin by finely chopping the onion and garlic. Heat a large skillet or pot, add oil, the chopped onion and garlic and sauté until soft.

Add the tomato purée and thyme and sauté for another minute.

Add the chopped tomatoes as well as the broth and leave the sauce to simmer.

Meanwhile, grate the squash with a grater. Use a clean kitchen towel to wring out the grated squash—this will ensure that the lasagna doesn't turn watery.

Once your tomato sauce is nearly ready, add the grated squash and stir.

Tip: You can easily make the tomato sauce ahead of time, as it only gets better the longer it's left to simmer.

Continued...

...continued

Next, prepare the bechamel sauce.

Béchamel sauce

Begin by melting the butter in a saucepan. Add flour and use a whisk to stir continuously until a smooth paste forms.

Gradually add the milk, stirring constantly until the sauce reaches the desired consistency. Season it with the nutmeg, salt, and pepper to taste.

Lasagna

Preheat the oven to 350°F.

Grate your halloumi or cut it into thin slices.

Now it's time to assemble your lasagna. Begin by adding a small amount of tomato sauce to the bottom of a baking dish. Add a layer of lasagna sheets, then tomato sauce, béchamel sauce, and finally halloumi. Repeat the layers until you run out or until you reach the top of the dish.

Place the lasagna in the oven.

After about 20 minutes, take out the lasagna and add grated mozzarella. Place it back in the oven for another 10–15 minutes.

Once finished, leave the lasagna to set for 5 minutes, then serve and enjoy!

Spaghetti Carbonara

Serves 2

Is it wrong to add cream to a Carbonara? Traditionally speaking, yes. But since I've removed the pancetta and replaced it with halloumi anyway, I think I can safely say that this Carbonara recipe is anything but traditional.

1 (200 g / 7 oz) block halloumi
3 egg yolks
1 cup grated parmesan
10 oz (300 g) spaghetti noodles
⅓ cup heavy cream
1–2 cloves garlic, pressed
Salt and pepper

Begin by cutting your halloumi into small chunks. Fry them in a pan until golden brown and crispy.

In a bowl, add the egg yolks and three-quarters of the parmesan and whisk together well.

In a large pot, bring water to a boil and cook the spaghetti according to the instructions on the package.

Remove the fried halloumi from the pan. Use the same pan to heat the cream along with the pressed garlic.

Add the cooked spaghetti to the pan along with cream, halloumi, and the egg and cheese mixture.

Stir it all together and finish by seasoning with salt and pepper to taste.

Top with the remaining parmesan, serve and enjoy!

From My Family to Yours

Chicken and Asparagus Tartlets

Serves 4

Chicken tartlets have always been my mother's favorite, and they are a cherished part of my childhood. After I stopped eating meat, I had to find a new way to make them and fortunately, I succeeded. Normally I would buy the tart shells ready-made, but for this book I wanted to try making them myself.

Tart shells

1 puff pastry sheet
1 egg

Filling

2 Tbsp butter
2 Tbsp wheat flour
1¼ cups vegetable broth
1 can white asparagus (save the drained liquid)
⅓ cup milk
⅓ cup heavy cream
1 (200 g / 7 oz) block halloumi
1 bundle green asparagus
1 egg
Pea shoots for garnish
Salt and pepper

Tart shells

Preheat the oven to 400°F.

On a flour-dusted work surface, roll out the puff pastry sheet.

Cut out circles using four oven-safe cups or tart moulds.

If using cups, line the outside of each cup with butter and place upside down.

Shape the cut-out dough pieces around the cups so that they take the shape of a tartlet. If using a mould, line with butter and press a piece of dough evenly into each mould. Brush with beaten egg.

Place the shells in the oven for approximately 8 minutes.

Once they're done baking, remove the shells from the cups, turn them right-side up, and brush the inside with beaten egg once more. Place them back in the oven for another 8 minutes or until they turn golden brown.

Continued…

...continued

Filling

Begin by melting the butter in a saucepan. Slowly add the flour and use a whisk to stir continuously until a smooth paste forms.

Slowly whisk in the broth until combined. Next, add ¾ cup of the water from the canned white asparagus and stir.

Add the milk and cream until a creamy consistency is reached and bring the sauce to a boil. Meanwhile, prepare the halloumi by cutting it into ¼-inch pieces. Fry them in a pan until golden brown and crispy.

Cut the green asparagus into bite-sized pieces and boil them in lightly salted water for about a minute.

Cut the canned white asparagus into bite-sized pieces.

Mix the white and green asparagus and the crispy halloumi with the sauce. Finish by seasoning with salt and pepper to taste.

To serve the tartlets, simply fill them with the sauce, garnish with pea shoots and enjoy!

Burning Love

Serves 2

While this dish is not named after the international hit song by Elvis Presley, it is every bit as classic. Just as the name would suggest, this simple and hearty Danish staple will leave you feeling warm and fuzzy, and—much like an old flame—it's a dish I always find myself coming back to.

1½ lb (800 g) potatoes
1 onion
1 (200 g / 7 oz) block halloumi
1 tsp paprika (optional)
⅓ cup butter
½ cup milk
3–4 small pickled beetroots
1 bunch chives
Salt and pepper

Begin by peeling the potatoes. Place them in a pot with salted water and boil for about 20 minutes or until tender.

Meanwhile, chop up the onion and dice the halloumi.

Fry the halloumi in a pan until golden brown and crispy.

Once ready, remove from the pan and place on a piece of paper towel to cool.

Add 2 tablespoons of the butter to the pan and fry your onions along with the paprika (optional).

Finely chop the chives and cut the pickled beetroot into bite-sized pieces.

Once the potatoes are tender, drain the water from the pot and add the milk along with the remaining butter. Using a masher or electric mixer, mash the potatoes to your desired consistency and finish by seasoning with salt and pepper to taste.

To serve, simply top the mashed potatoes with fried onions, halloumi, and pickled beetroot and garnish with chives. Enjoy!

Fortsættes

Hash Béarnaise

Serves 2

I have recently become aware that I do not cook hash nearly as often as I would like, and as a result I have started to keep extra potatoes handy for just such an occasion. Because, in my book, a lunch doesn't get much better than a hearty potato hash topped with béarnaise.

Potato hash
1⅓ lb (600 g) potatoes
1 onion
2 Tbsp butter
1 (200 g / 7 oz) block halloumi

Béarnaise essence
1 shallot
1 bunch tarragon, chopped
3 Tbsp white wine vinegar
3 Tbsp water

Potato hash

Begin by chopping up your potatoes and onion.

In a pan, add butter and fry the potatoes and onions until tender and golden brown.

Meanwhile, cut your halloumi into pieces as big or small as you'd like. Fry them in a separate pan with oil until golden brown and crispy.

Béarnaise essence

Finely chop the shallot and place it in a pot along with a handful of the tarragon, the white wine vinegar, and water. Bring it to a boil and let it cook until you're left with about 3 tablespoons of liquid. Strain out the onion and tarragon, leaving only the essence. Set aside.

Continued…

…continued

Béarnaise sauce

¾ cup butter
Béarnaise essence
3 egg yolks
½ lemon
Salt and pepper

Toppings

2 eggs
2 pickled beetroots or pickled red onions
Garden cress for garnish

Béarnaise sauce

Begin by melting the butter in a small saucepan.

Once it's melted, you'll notice that a white residue has collected at the bottom of the saucepan. Carefully pour the clear fat into a bowl, leaving the white residue behind.

Heat up the béarnaise essence. Add the egg yolks to the pot while whisking continuously to keep the mixture from separating. Keep going until the mixture thickens.

Next, slowly add the clarified butter while whisking constantly. If needed, remove the pot from the heat now and again.

Continue whisking until all the clarified butter has been incorporated into the sauce. Finish by seasoning with salt, pepper, and fresh tarragon to taste.

Toppings

Before serving, fry up the eggs in a pan and cut the pickled beetroots or pickled red onions into smaller pieces. (You'll find a recipe for pickled red onions on page 101.)

To serve, mix together the fried potatoes, onions, halloumi, and toppings—and don't skimp on the béarnaise. Enjoy!

Halloumi Meatballs with Scalloped Potatoes

Serves 4

One of my fondest childhood memories is of spending the day at my grandparents' house and stuffing my face with Grandma's homemade meatballs until I could barely walk. Although I can no longer enjoy her meatballs, I wanted to honor her memory by creating my own version of her wonderful recipe.

Scalloped potatoes
4½ lb (2 kg) potatoes
3 leeks
2 cloves garlic
3 cups heavy cream
¾ cup cream cheese
Salt and pepper

Halloumi meatballs
1 squash
2 large carrots
1 (200 g / 7 oz) block halloumi
1 shallot
1 egg
2 Tbsp butter
Salt and pepper

Scalloped potatoes

Preheat the oven to 375°F.

Begin by peeling and cutting the potatoes into evenly sized slices. I used a mandoline slicer to make ultrafine slices, but a knife works just as well. Layer the potatoes however you'd like in a baking dish—I stacked mine upright, but it's quicker to simply lay them flat.

Rinse the leeks thoroughly and chop them up along with the garlic. Fry them in a heated pan with oil.

Add the heavy cream to the pan along with the cream cheese and bring it to a boil. Season to taste with salt and pepper.

Once the sauce has reached a creamy consistency, pour it over the potatoes and place the baking dish in the oven for about 1 hour. Check on the potatoes regularly to ensure they don't burn.

Meanwhile, prepare your halloumi meatballs.

Continued...

...continued

Halloumi meatballs

Begin by grating the squash and carrots. Use a clean kitchen towel to wring out the grated vegetables.

Next, grate the halloumi and mix it with the vegetables in a bowl.

Finely chop the shallot and add it to the bowl.

Add the egg, and mix. Season to taste with salt and pepper.

Now it's time to shape the meatballs. Feel free to make them as big or small as you want. Heat up a pan, add butter and fry the meatballs until brown and crispy on the outside.

Once the meatballs and the scalloped potatoes are finished, simply serve and enjoy!

Fried "Pork Belly" with Potatoes

Serves 2

When I became a vegetarian this meat-heavy dish pretty much disappeared from my life, until one fateful day when my girlfriend accidentally fried the halloumi for too long. The result was perfectly crispy as fried pork belly should be, and just like that, I was able to reunite with this Danish classic.

Potatoes and fried "pork belly"

1⅓ lb (600 g) new potatoes
2 (200 g / 7 oz each) blocks halloumi

Parsley sauce

1 bunch parsley
2 Tbsp butter
2 Tbsp wheat flour
1½ cups milk
Juice of ½ lemon
Salt and pepper

Potatoes and fried "pork belly"

Begin by cleaning your new potatoes. Then place them in a pot with salted water and boil until tender.

Meanwhile, cut both halloumi blocks into 8 equal-size patties, making 16 in total. Heat a pan, add butter, and fry the halloumi until brown and crispy. They may need a bit more time in the pan to ensure that perfect crispy crust—almost like fried pieces of pork.

Parsley sauce

Rinse and finely chop the parsley. Set aside.

Melt the butter in a pan. Slowly add flour and use a whisk to stir continuously until a smooth paste forms.

Gradually add the milk, stirring constantly until the sauce reaches the desired consistency.

Finally, add the parsley and season with the lemon, salt, and pepper to taste.

Once the potatoes are cooked and the halloumi is crispy, serve both along with a side of parsley sauce. Enjoy!

Savory Egg and Leek Pie

Serves 2

Whenever we went to a family potluck, my mother would bring her signature egg and leek pie. This evergreen dish is a sure winner every time—but don't just take my word for it!

1 pie dough
1 (200 g / 7 oz) block halloumi
6 leeks
4 eggs
¾ cup heavy cream
1 tsp fresh thyme
¼ cup sun-dried tomatoes, drained
½ cup grated mozzarella
Salt and pepper

Tip: Unless you prefer to make your own pie dough, you can easily use a store-bought version if you're pressed for time.

Preheat the oven to 350°F.

Cut your halloumi into pieces about ¼ inch long/wide. Fry them in a pan until golden brown and crispy.

Rinse the leeks thoroughly and chop them into thin rings.

In a bowl, whisk together the eggs, heavy cream, thyme, sun-dried tomatoes, mozzarella, and halloumi. Add salt and pepper to taste.

Grease a pie plate and roll your dough over and into the plate.

Add the leek rings, then pour in the egg mixture.

Place the pie in the oven for approximately 25 minutes.

Serve with greens or a salad on the side and enjoy!

Spaghetti No-Meatballs

Serves 2

Spaghetti and meatballs is perhaps more of a Disney classic than a family one, but it's close enough in my book—and truthfully, I would take this halloumi version over a classic meat sauce any day.

Tomato sauce

1 onion
2 cloves garlic
1 tsp paprika
2 Tbsp tomato purée
2 (540 mL / 19 oz) cans chopped tomatoes
1 handful fresh basil

"Meatballs"

1 (200 g / 7 oz) block halloumi
2 carrots
1 egg
1 handful fresh basil
1 tsp paprika
4 Tbsp wheat flour
Salt and pepper
4 cups neutral cooking oil for deep-frying

½ cup parmesan
Basil for garnish

Tomato sauce

Begin by chopping up the onion and garlic. Heat a large skillet or pot. Add oil, the chopped onion and garlic and sauté until soft. Next, add the paprika and tomato purée and sauté for another minute.

Finally, add the two cans of chopped tomatoes and the fresh basil and leave the sauce to simmer while you prepare your "meatballs."

"Meatballs"

Begin by grating halloumi and carrots with a grater.

Place both in a bowl, add the rest of the meatball ingredients and mix well.

Roll the stuffing into meatballs as big or small as you'd like.

Bring a pot of salted water to a boil. Add the spaghetti and leave it to cook while you deep-fry your meatballs.

In a pot or deep saucepan, heat cooking oil to 350°F. Once it's ready, carefully place the "meatballs" in the oil to deep-fry. Once they start to brown, remove and place them on a piece of paper towel to drain excess oil.

To serve, plate the spaghetti with the "meatballs" and tomato sauce on top along with freshly grated parmesan. Garnish with fresh basil and enjoy!

Open-Faced Potato Sandwich

Serves 2

One of the best-known dishes in Danish cuisine consists of a loaded open-faced sandwich—or smørrebrød, as it's called—with various toppings. After living abroad for a few years, you really learn to appreciate the simplicity and versatility of smørrebrød, and this is one of my all-time favorites.

Potatoes
10 oz (300 g) new potatoes

Pickled red onions
1 red onion
½ cup vinegar
½ cup water
¼ cup white sugar

Herb mayonnaise
1 bunch chives
1½ cups neutral cooking oil
2 egg yolks
1 Tbsp mustard
1 Tbsp white wine vinegar
Salt and pepper

Potatoes

Begin by boiling your potatoes until tender.

Pickled red onions

Cut the red onion into thin rings and place them in a jam jar.

In a saucepan, combine the vinegar, water, and sugar and bring to a boil. Once it's boiling, pour it over the red onion rings. Place the jar in the fridge to cool until serving time.

Herb mayonnaise

Using an immersion blender, blend the chives very finely and mix in the neutral cooking oil.

In a bowl, mix the egg yolks with the mustard and white wine vinegar.

Slowly add the chive oil to the bowl while whisking continuously, until the mayo has reached the desired consistency. Season with salt and pepper to taste.

Continued...

...continued

Breaded halloumi

1 (200 g / 7 oz) block halloumi
1½ cups wheat flour
2 eggs
1½ cups panko breadcrumbs
4 cups neutral cooking oil

4 slices of good-quality bread, preferably rye or whole grain
Salt and pepper

Breaded halloumi

Divide the flour, eggs, and breadcrumbs into separate bowls—one for each ingredient.

Cut your halloumi into ½-inch pieces.

Bread each piece in the following order: wheat flour, eggs, and finally breadcrumbs. Feel free to add another coat of egg and breadcrumbs.

In a pot or deep saucepan, heat the cooking oil to 350°F.

Next, carefully place the breaded halloumi pieces in the oil and deep-fry them until golden brown and crispy.

Now it's time to assemble the sandwich. First, spread some of the herb mayo onto each slice of bread, then add the sliced potatoes. Next, place a few pieces of the crispy halloumi on top of the potatoes. Finish by garnishing with the pickled red onions and enjoy!

Winter Warmers

Cozy Curry Pot

Serves 2

This winter dish is what you might call a happy accident, as it came to be when I was in the process of making another dish which sadly came out completely wrong. However, it became the starting point for this wonderful curry pot that's perfect for a cozy winter evening.

2 onions
2–3 cloves garlic
1 tsp ginger
2 Tbsp curry powder
1 Tbsp cumin
1 Tbsp paprika
2 (400 mL / 13.5 oz) cans coconut milk
2 vegetable stock cubes (I use Knorr)
1 red bell pepper
1 (540 mL / 19 oz) can of chickpeas
1 cauliflower
1 (200 g / 7 oz) block halloumi
½ lemon

Begin by finely chopping the onions and garlic. Heat a large skillet or pot. Add oil, the chopped onion and garlic, and sauté until soft.

Add the ginger, curry powder, cumin, and paprika and sauté for another minute.

Next, add the two cans of coconut milk along with the vegetable stock cubes and leave to simmer.

Chop the red pepper into pieces and add it to the pot.

Rinse the chickpeas and set aside.

Cut the cauliflower into small florets, or large patties if preferred.

In a pan, add butter and fry up the cauliflower pieces until they turn crispy around the edges. Place them in the oven and continue to bake at 325°F until the rest of the dish is ready.

Cut the halloumi into slices and fry them in a pan until golden brown and crispy.

5 minutes before the halloumi is ready, add the chickpeas to the curry pot.

Once the halloumi is ready, remove the cauliflower from the oven and place on a plate.

To serve, simply pour the contents of the curry pot over the cauliflower, top with halloumi, and enjoy!

Halloumi Stroganoff

Serves 2

There are about a million ways to make this dish depending on personal preferences and available ingredients. I like to use extra red lentils in mine and enjoy it as is. However, if you would like to add rice or mashed potatoes I recommend using only half the amount of red lentils listed here.

1 onion
2 carrots
¾ cup dried red lentils
2 Tbsp tomato purée
1 tsp dried thyme
1 (540 mL / 19 oz) can chopped tomatoes
1 vegetable stock cube
1 cup cooking cream
Salt and pepper
1 (200 g / 7 oz) block halloumi

Begin by finely chopping the onion and julienning the carrots.

Heat a large skillet or pot. Add oil and the chopped onion and sauté until soft. Add the carrots and continue to sauté.

In another pot, cook the red lentils according to the instructions on the package.

Add the tomato purée and dried thyme to the onions and carrots and let it heat up.

Next, add the chopped tomatoes and vegetable stock cube. Bring the pot to a boil.

Add the cream and continue to boil for a few minutes until combined. Season to taste with salt and pepper.

Cut your halloumi into 6 equal-size slices. Fry them in a pan until golden brown and crispy.

Just before the halloumi is ready, pour the cooked red lentils into the other pot and mix together.

Serve the stroganoff topped with crispy halloumi and enjoy!

Spicy Tomato Stew

Serves 2

When the cold winter air blows in, there's nothing quite like a hot stew to warm up with. This hearty dish makes for a spicy treat to enjoy on chilly days.

1 onion
3 cloves garlic
1 red pepper
1 tsp chili flakes
1 tsp paprika
1 tsp dried oregano
2 (540 mL / 19 oz) cans chopped tomatoes
1 (540 mL / 19 oz) can white beans
1 (200 g / 7 oz) block halloumi
Oregano for garnish

Begin by finely chopping the onion and garlic. Heat a large skillet or pot. Add oil, the chopped onion and garlic and sauté until soft.

Cut the pepper into thin strips and add them to the pot.

Add the spices and sauté for another minute.

Pour in the chopped tomatoes and boil for about 5 minutes.

Meanwhile, drain the liquid from the white beans and cut your halloumi into 6 equal-size pieces.

Preheat your oven to 400°F.

After leaving the stew to boil for 5 minutes, stir in the white beans. Pour the stew into a deep oven-safe dish.

Place your halloumi on top of the stew. Place the dish in the oven for about 20 minutes or until the halloumi is golden brown and crispy.

Serve while piping hot with a few pieces of crispy halloumi on top and enjoy!

"Roast Pork" Sandwich

Serves 2

It has taken me years to learn to truly appreciate a roast pork sandwich, but after trying one at a local football concession stand I knew had to make some myself—and I would argue that this pork-free version rivals the original.

Brown sauce (optional)

¼ cup butter
4 Tbsp flour
1½ cups vegetable broth
½ cup cream
Gravy browning
Salt and pepper

"Roast pork" sandwich

¾ cup flour
1 egg
¾ cup panko breadcrumbs
4 cups neutral cooking oil
1 (200 g / 7 oz) block halloumi
¼ red cabbage
Pickled cucumbers
2 burger buns (I prefer brioche)
2 Tbsp mayonnaise

Brown sauce (optional)

Begin by melting the butter in a pan. Slowly add the flour while stirring continuously to form a paste.

Slowly add the broth while stirring. Lastly, add the cream and stir. You can adjust the consistency to your taste by adding water.

Leave the sauce to simmer while you prepare the rest—but remember to stir it frequently.

"Roast pork" sandwich

Divide the flour, egg, and breadcrumbs into separate bowls—one for each ingredient.

Cut the halloumi into 2 pieces along the middle as if they were steaks, and bread them in the following order: flour, egg, breadcrumbs, egg, and breadcrumbs.

In a deep pot, pour in the oil and heat it to 350°F. This will be used to deep-fry your halloumi.

While waiting for the oil to heat up, finely chop the red cabbage and slice the pickled cucumbers.

Continued...

...continued

Once the oil is ready, carefully add your halloumi pieces and deep-fry them until golden brown and crispy.

Heat your burger buns in the oven so that they're ready for assembling.

Stir the sauce once more. Season with salt and pepper to taste and add gravy browning.

Once the halloumi is crispy, remove from the oil and place on a piece of paper towel to soak up excess oil while you prepare the sandwich.

Remove the burger buns from the oven, cut them in half, and spread a tablespoon of mayonnaise on each lower half. Next, add finely chopped red cabbage, halloumi, and pickled cucumbers.

Finish by pouring brown sauce over the sandwich, serve and enjoy!

Winter Salad with Carrots and Parsnips

Serves 2

Another cherished childhood memory of mine, this wonderful winter salad uses seasonal ingredients and is a perfect side. The addition of halloumi makes it a great stand-alone meal as well.

Pickled pearl onions

1 lb (500 g) pearl onions
¾ cup white vinegar
⅓ cup honey
1¼ cup water
2 sprigs of thyme
10 black peppercorns
1 tsp of salt

Mint dressing

½ cucumber
½ cup yogurt
10 mint leaves, finely chopped
Salt and pepper

Pickled pearl onions

Prepare your pearl onions by peeling them and cutting off the tops and bottoms. Place them in a pickle jar. Combine white vinegar and the remaining ingredients in a pot and bring it to a boil. Once boiling, pour it into the picke jar and place the onions in the fridge. They can easily be made a day or two ahead of time.

Mint dressing

Grate the cucumber and use a clean kitchen towel to wring out excess liquid. Mix well with the yogurt.

Add the mint, salt, and pepper to taste. Store the dressing in the refrigerator until serving time.

Continued…

...continued

Winter salad

1 onion
4 carrots
1 parsnip
1 beetroot
2–3 cloves garlic, peeled
3 Tbsp olive oil
1 Tbsp dried thyme
Salt and pepper
1 (200 g / 7 oz) block halloumi

Winter salad

Chop the onions, carrots, parsnips, and beetroot into large oblong pieces.

Preheat the oven to 400°F.

Place all your vegetables and whole cloves of garlic on a baking tray. Pour oil over the vegetables and sprinkle the dried thyme, salt, and pepper. Toss to coat.

Roast the vegetables in the oven for about 30–35 minutes. Check on them throughout—I recommend tossing and rotating them halfway through.

Cut your halloumi into long strips and fry them in a pan until golden brown and crispy.

Once the vegetables are ready, simply serve with the halloumi, pickled pearl onions, and mint dressing on top. Enjoy!

Indian Tikka Masala

Serves 2

My girlfriend deserves full credit for the inclusion of this dish. Back when we started dating, I rarely if ever cooked Indian dishes. Needless to say, I have since made up for lost time. This classic recipe is the perfect introduction to the flavorful world of Indian cuisine.

1 onion
3 cloves garlic
1 Tbsp grated ginger
1 Tbsp garam masala
1 tsp chili flakes
1 (540 mL / 19 oz) can chopped tomatoes
¾ cup cooking cream
¾ cup jasmine rice
1 (200 g / 7 oz) block halloumi
Naan bread (optional)
Salt and pepper
⅔ cup cashew nuts

Begin by finely chopping the onion and garlic. Heat a large skillet or pot. Add oil, the chopped onion and garlic and sauté until soft. Add the grated ginger, garam masala, and chili flakes and sauté for 1 minute.

Add the chopped tomatoes and cream and bring to a boil—taste and adjust the seasoning as you go.

Meanwhile, in another pot, cook your rice according to the instructions on the package.

Cut the halloumi into large chunks and fry them in a pan until golden brown and crispy.

If you're serving the dish with naan bread, now's the time to heat it.

Finish by seasoning your masala with salt and pepper to taste. Serve with crispy halloumi, a side of rice, and crushed cashew nuts sprinkled on top. Enjoy!

Thai Peanut Curry

Serves 2

This Thai recipe is based on one of the many dishes I brought home from my time in Sydney, Australia. During my internship, I discovered a lovely Thai place just around the corner from work, and it quickly became my go-to whenever I felt like treating myself.

4 oz (120 g) spring onions (save some for garnishing)
7 oz (200 g) sugar snap peas
1 red bell pepper
1 yellow pepper
1 (200 g / 7 oz) block halloumi
1 tsp ginger
4 Tbsp sweet chili sauce
2 Tbsp soy sauce
3 Tbsp peanut butter
1½ cups coconut milk
Juice of 1 lime
10 oz (300 g) egg noodles
1 tsp chili flakes
⅓ cup peanuts

Begin by cutting the spring onions, sugar snap peas, and peppers into thin strips.

In a wok or deep pan, heat up some oil and fry the vegetables.

Cut your halloumi into long strips and add them to the wok. Continue to fry until the halloumi is nice and crispy.

Next, add the ginger, chili sauce, soy sauce, and peanut butter to the pan and mix well.

Once mixed, add the coconut milk and lime juice and mix once more.

Turn down the heat and let the curry simmer until it reaches a creamy consistency.

Meanwhile, cook the egg noodles according to the instructions on the package.

Once cooked, add the noodles to the curry along with chili flakes and mix well.

To serve, simply plate the curry with the remaining spring onions and the peanuts sprinkled on top and enjoy!

Chili sin Carne

Serves 2

Chili con carne has always been a favorite among me and my friends whenever we've invited each other over for dinner, because it's easy to make in large batches – plus, everyone loves a good chili. Thankfully, I can still invite my friends over for this delicious Chili sin Carne.

2 onions
2 cloves garlic
2 bell peppers
2 Tbsp tomato purée
¾ cup red lentils
1 fresh chili
1 handful thyme
1 tsp cinnamon
2 Tbsp paprika
2 (540 mL / 19 oz) cans chopped tomatoes
1 (540 mL / 19 oz) can mixed beans
1 (200 g / 7 oz) block halloumi
1 square dark chocolate
Juice of ½ lemon
Salt and pepper
½ cup crème fraîche

Begin by chopping the onion and pressing the garlic. Heat a large skillet or pot. Add oil, the chopped onion and the garlic and sauté until soft.

Cut the bell peppers into small pieces and add them to the pot along with the tomato purée, red lentils, chili, thyme, cinnamon, and paprika. Leave it to simmer for a minute.

Add the chopped tomatoes and beans and mix well.

Let it simmer for about 45 minutes—or longer if you have the time.

Meanwhile, cut the halloumi into large squares and fry them in a pan until golden brown and crispy.

Just before serving, add the halloumi and dark chocolate to the chili. Finish by seasoning with the lemon juice, salt, and pepper to taste.

Plate your chili with a dollop of crème fraîche on top and a side of rice or nachos, serve and enjoy!

Creamy Sunchoke Soup

Serves 2

Soup is a staple in our household. One of our favorites is this rich and creamy soup made with sunchokes—also known as Jerusalem artichokes—which is perfect for a cold winter's day. Combined with crispy chips and halloumi, it's a sure win every time.

Sunchoke chips

3 sunchokes
2 cups neutral cooking oil
Salt

Soup

1 lb (500 g) sunchokes
12 oz (350 g) potatoes
1 onion
2 cloves garlic
3 sprigs fresh thyme
4 cups vegetable broth
1 (200 g / 7 oz) block halloumi
½ cup heavy cream
Juice of ½ lemon
Salt and pepper

Sunchoke Chips

Begin by peeling the sunchokes. Slice them into very thin chips—I use a mandoline slicer. Pat them dry with paper towel or a clean kitchen towel.

In a deep pot, heat up the oil. When it reaches approximately 350°F, carefully place your sunchoke chips in the pot to deep-fry. Once they've turned brown and crispy, place them on a piece of paper towel to soak up excess oil. Finish by sprinkling a bit of salt on top.

Soup

Peel the sunchokes and potatoes and cut them into small chunks.

Finely chop the onion and garlic. Sauté in a large skillet or pot along with oil. Add the sunchokes, potatoes, and thyme sprigs and sauté for a few more minutes.

Next, add the broth and leave to boil for about 25 minutes, until the potatoes and sunchokes are tender.

Meanwhile, cut your halloumi into small ¼-inch cubes. Fry them in a pan until golden brown and crispy.

Fish the thyme sprigs out of the soup. Use a blender to purée the soup until smooth, add the heavy cream and bring the soup to a boil once more. Finish by seasoning with the lemon juice, salt, and pepper to taste.

Serve with sunchoke chips and halloumi and enjoy!

Acknowledgments

There are many who I'd like to thank for making this book possible. Firstly, I would like to thank my wonderful girlfriend who first introduced me to halloumi, and who has since had to endure countless taste testings of various halloumi dishes.

I would also like to thank Hanne from Muusmann Forlag for being on board with the idea right from the start, as well as being an invaluable source of inspiration throughout the entire process.

Another big thank you goes out to my incredibly talented photographer, Anne Marie Jo, who has been phenomenal to work with and perfectly captured my visions and ideas. Without her, this book would not have been the same.

The same applies to my fantastic food stylist Ditte Dalsgaard Nielsen who, alongside Anne Marie, elevated my dishes beyond what I had ever dared to hope for.

Last but not least, a huge thank you to all who have bought the book. It means the world to me that you want to share in my knowledge of and love for halloumi.

Plates

A special thanks to all of the wonderful brands who so kindly lent me their beautiful plates and allowed me to capture and frame each of my dishes exactly like I had envisioned.

Villeroy & Boch
Rörstrand
Gien
Iittala
Kockums
Ann Demeulemeester
Pillivuyt
Olsson & Jensen
Ginori 1735
Sakura Copenhagen
Lexington
Spode
Mateus
Götefors Porslin
Le Creuset
Sagaform
Marimekko
Rosendahl
By On

Index

P

Q

R

S

About the Author

Rasmus Zepernick is passionate about sharing his love for halloumi with the world, and in doing so he created this book. For the past several years, he has made and remade countless dishes with halloumi as the centerpiece, and this book serves as a comprehensive collection of his all-time favorites.

Originally published in Denmark in 2022 by Muusmann Forlag, Copenhagen, as *Halloumi: Osten, der vil smelte dit hjerte* (ISBN: 9788794086981)

Interior design: Muusmann Forlag

Photos: Anne Marie Jo

Food stylist: Ditte Dalsgaard Nielsen

Typesetting of English edition: Sydney Barnes

TouchWood Editions
touchwoodeditions.com

CATALOGUING DATA AVAILABLE FROM LIBRARY AND ARCHIVES CANADA
ISBN 9781771514460 (hardcover)
ISBN 9781771514477 (electronic)

TouchWood Editions acknowledges that the land on which we live and work is within the traditional territories of the Lkwungen (Esquimalt and Songhees), Malahat, Pacheedaht, Scia'new, T'Sou-ke and W̱SÁNEĆ (Pauquachin, Tsartlip, Tsawout, Tseycum) peoples.

We acknowledge the financial support of the Government of Canada through the Canada Book Fund, and of the Province of British Columbia through the Book Publishing Tax Credit.

This book was produced using FSC®-certified, acid-free papers, processed chlorine free, and printed with soya-based inks.

Printed in China

28 27 26 25 24 1 2 3 4 5